Contents

Introduction

ABOUT THIS SERIES

Photographs are hugely influential in all our lives. Every day we are exposed to hundreds of images, from the cereal packet we see at breakfast, to advertisements, newspaper photographs, and shop window displays. Images like these play an important role in shaping our ideas about ourselves and other people.

However, the pictures we see do not always tell the whole story. Media representations of countries of the South can often contribute to negative stereotypes. It is important that children, as well as adults, learn to question photographs. Visual literacy can be as important as print literacy when it comes to getting the most out of today's information-rich environment.

Oxfam and photographs

Oxfam Development Education has many years of experience in working with photographs in the primary classroom. Using good quality photographs which offer an alternative perspective can help even very young children to develop an informed view of the world around them.

As an international development agency, Oxfam has the opportunity and responsibility to communicate the reality of everyday life for people in the South. Our photographers work with partner organisations and individuals in the South to produce images which reflect this reality. We let people know that the photos will be used to communicate with audiences in the UK and elsewhere, as part of Oxfam's commitment to campaigning and advocacy.

Over many years, Oxfam has collected a huge library of photographs from around the world, which we would like to make available for classroom use. *Photo Opportunities Science* is the second in a series where our education staff select photographs for use in a specific area of the curriculum.

The aims of the *Photo Opportunities* series are:

- to extend opportunities for teachers to use a range of photographs from both North and South in all curriculum areas

- to give children a broader perspective on the world, and enable them to make links between their own lives and the lives of others

- to promote a Development Education approach by encouraging active learning and cooperative group work.

CHOOSING AND USING PHOTOGRAPHS

Many children will be used to looking at photos of friends and family, and most children will already be familiar with having their picture taken. (They will understand that this is not always a positive experience!) The immediacy and familiarity of photos as a medium may suggest that working with them in the classroom is straightforward. However, visual literacy is a skill that needs to be taught, and working with photos should not be seen as an easy option. It is important to be clear why photos are being used, and how they fit in with the rest of the work that the pupils are doing.

Photos can be a good way to introduce a new topic, such as families or homes. They are useful in establishing a baseline of knowledge and understanding that children might already have about another place, or other people's lives. They can provide a neutral starting point, a forum in which children can begin to share, discuss, and question their ideas with confidence. Pupils should be given the opportunity to discuss photos without feeling that they might be giving the 'wrong' answer or opinion. Remember that different children will interact with and interpret each photo very differently – in just the same way as they would react when meeting someone for the first time. A child's expectations, experiences, and preconceptions will inform their understanding.

Schools use photos in many different ways, and it is worth considering where and how photos are used, both in the classroom and outside it. For example, what sort of images does the school use in its own publicity material?

How do children respond to and 'read' photos? Do they see what adults see?

Research* has shown that when children look at photographs, they are probably not 'seeing' what adults assume they see. This means it is important to use activities that help children to look carefully and critically at different parts of the photo, as well as at the photo as a whole.

- Children will 'home in' on clues in the picture that seem familiar and use these to interpret the photo – even if their understanding of the clue doesn't fit the context of the rest of the picture.

- Children may add details that aren't there at all. They may 'see' things that are associated with what they feel about the photo, based on their existing knowledge and preconceptions.

- Children respond differently to photographs according to their age. Young children find detail very important; older children concentrate more on the overall themes of the picture. Younger children may not notice the middle ground of the picture, and will look more at the foreground and background.

- Children will tend to ignore the unfamiliar.

*Margaret Mackintosh, 'Learning from Photographs', in *Primary Sources: Research findings in Primary Geography*, the Geographical Association, 1998.

Checklist

- Work with photos should be integrated with other classroom work.

- Start with photos of people and places that children are familiar with, before moving on to less familiar subjects.

- Use photos of a good technical quality.

- Put photos in some sort of context. Why was the photo taken? Who by? What for?

- Give children as much accurate information as possible about the people and places in the photos you use.

- Encourage children to explore the links between their own lives and experiences and those of the people in the photos.

Finding out more about people and places

Using an enquiry-based approach to work with photos will generate lots of questions. This may seem daunting at first, but, with support from adults, children are capable of researching information and drawing their own conclusions.

One technique to draw out areas for further investigation is to stick a photo onto a large blank sheet of paper. As a whole class or in small groups, brainstorm questions you would like to know the answers to, and write them down around the photo. Next, sort the questions according to whether they are matters of fact ('What is the weather like in India?') or opinion ('What is Shakeel thinking about?'). Brainstorm ways in which you could find the answers to your questions. Are there some questions which will be more difficult to answer than others? Are there any clues in the picture which could help suggest some answers?

Information sources

- Encyclopedias, atlases, and dictionaries

- Textbooks and photopacks

- Websites

- Internet discussion boards and e-mail groups

- CD ROMs

- Tourist brochures

- Newspapers and magazines

- Charities and NGOs

- Embassies

- Friends and relatives

- Link schools in other countries or regions

WHY USE PHOTOGRAPHS TO TEACH SCIENCE?

Science is all around us in our everyday lives, but we don't always know it. One advantage of using photographs is that children can connect science to everyday activities such as cooking or looking after plants and animals. Far from being removed from everyday life, science can become more accessible to children once they realise that we draw on scientific knowledge all the time as we live our lives. By using these photos of people in different countries, mostly drawn from Oxfam's extensive collection, children can recognise that people the world over have the same needs (for food and water for example) and are engaged in similar activities. They will learn that science is universal. For children whose origins may not be in the UK, the use of images from other countries will give value to their own backgrounds and contribute to the development of their self-esteem. In certain circumstances, they may be able to share their experiences with the whole class.

Children will be able to see that although life in other countries may differ in terms of facilities, climate and customs, there are also many similarities with their own lives. The photographs have been chosen to link with various areas of science, leading to practical activities that the children can carry out for themselves. It may be appropriate to use the photographs to introduce a topic, but they can also be used at any time, to introduce a different dimension, or to broaden the topic of science being investigated. Some of the photographs are linked to the same area of science so that they form a set of teaching activities, while some photographs are suitable for use for more than one topic area.

Although the photographs have been selected with science in mind, they will also provide links from science to other curriculum areas such as geography, design and technology or citizenship.

Photography can be used in schools as a way of recording work in science. If appropriate, children should be encouraged to take photographs of their own work; otherwise the teacher can take pictures of the work at different stages. For young children, photographs provide an effective *aide-mémoire* to help them recall what they did during a science investigation, so that they are able to put a record of their findings into a chronological sequence.

Each of the photographs accompanies a unit of study which suggests discussion points, activities and practical investigations suitable for children in years 1 and 2. Perhaps the most important activity of all should be talking – discussions between the teacher and children, and children talking to each other in small groups. All the teacher's notes suggest suitable questions for prompting discussion, but it is also important that children are able to ask their own questions, as this will help them to engage more fully with the photographs. All the practical activities have been chosen to link with the science curriculum for this age range, while also bringing a global dimension into the classroom wherever possible. Some background information about each photograph has been provided at the beginning of the teacher's book, so that the teacher can make use of it wherever it seems relevant. The children can then gain some familiarity with the countries shown, and increase their awareness of the wider world.

CURRICULUM LINKS

The activities in the pack have been closely linked to the science curriculum, covering the following attainment targets.

England

Attainment target, Key Stage 1		*Unit*
Sc1 Scientific enquiry	2a Ask questions and decide how they might find answers to them	All units
	2c Think about what might happen before deciding what to do	
	2g Communicate what happened in a variety of ways	
	2i Compare what happened with what they expected would happen	
Sc2 Life processes and living things	1a Learn the differences between things that are living and things have never been alive	3,6,7,8
	2b Learn that humans and other animals need food and water to stay alive	8,9
	2c Learn that taking exercise and eating the right types and amounts of food help humans to keep healthy	9
	2e Learn how to treat animals with care and sensitivity	
	3a Recognise that plants need light and water to grow	5,6,7
	3c Learn that seeds grow into flowering plants	5,6
	4a Recognise similarities and differences between themselves and others, and to treat others with sensitivity	10
	5c Learn to care for the environment	7

Sc3 Materials and their properties	1d Find out about the uses of a variety of materials and how these are chosen for specific uses on the basis of their simple properties	12
	2b Explore and describe the way some everyday materials change when they are heated or cooled	11
Sc4 Physical processes	2a Find out about, and describe the movement of familiar things	4
	2b Learn that both pushes and pulls are examples of forces	4
	3a Identify different light sources including the sun	3
	3b Learn that darkness is the absence of light	3
	3c Learn that there are many kinds of sound and sources of sound	3

Scotland

Attainment target	Strand	Unit
Earth and space level A	Link the pattern of day and night to the position of the sun	2
Changing materials level A	Describe how everyday materials can be changed by heating or cooling	11
Materials from Earth level A	Make simple observations of differences in the properties of common materials	12
	Relate the use of everyday materials to properties	12
Properties and uses of energy level A	Give examples of sources of heat light and sound	2, 3
	Give examples of everyday uses of heat light and sound	3, 11
level B	Link light to shadow formation	2
level C	Link sounds to sources of vibration	3
Conversion and transfer of energy level B	Link the intake of food to the movement of their body	9
Forces and their effects level A	Give examples of pushing and pulling	4
Living things level A	Sort living things into broad groups	8
The processes of life level A	Give the conditions needed by animals and plants in order to remain healthy	5, 6, 7, 8, 9, 10
level A	Recognise similarities and differences between themselves and others	10
level B	Recognise stages in the life cycles of familiar plants	5, 6
Interaction of living things with their environment level A	Give examples of how to care for living things and the environment	7, 8

Wales

Photo information for teachers

PHOTOCARDS

1 Shadows

This picture was taken in Turkana, northwest Kenya, a dry area inhabited by 'pastoralists', i.e. semi-nomadic people who live by herding livestock. They are finding it hard to survive with their traditional lifestyle. Scarcity of rain is a problem, and the people are finding that they are no longer able to move freely across their lands because of the increased threat of conflict. This has been exacerbated by inappropriate government policies and the easy availability of modern arms. Traditional patterns of mobility are breaking down, which makes people more vulnerable to drought. Social structures are also being disrupted, with Elders having less control over young people.

Crispin Hughes/Oxfam

2 Girl with drum

This girl, Elisa Samao aged nine, is pictured playing a drum at school. She is the youngest child in the family, and has older brothers and sisters who are now grown up. Unlike her, they did not have the chance to go to school because her father couldn't afford to pay the fees. Her sisters work in the fields with her parents, but she hopes to have a different kind of life. Her school was built in 1998. Elisa lives in Gurue in the northern half of Mozambique, not far from the border with Malawi.

Joel Chiziane/Oxfam

3 Boy with donkey

This boy comes from Ludovico village in Maranhão province in northeastern Brazil. The donkey is carrying a load of babassu nuts. These nuts, which are rich in oil, are grown in this area, and are the economic mainstay of local families. The oil is used to make soap, and there is a soap factory in the village. Many local women work in the factory. Children sometimes help to split the nuts in their spare time. Ludovico village appears in two previous publications, *Wake up, World!* (Frances Lincoln, in association with Oxfam 1999) and *Your World, My World* (Oxfam 2001). Both these books, for children at key stage 1 / P1-P3, feature a young Brazilian girl, Cidinha, and give details about her life in the village. The tree from which the nuts come is a type of palm tree.

Julio Etchart/Oxfam

4 Slicing a pumpkin

This picture was taken in the KwaZulu Natal province of South Africa. It shows a woman, Nomusa Shezi, preparing food. Pumpkins are one of the vegetables grown by local people in this poor, rural area of South Africa. Many of the men are migrant workers, while the women stay at home running the households and growing food. A typical dish would be *isijingi*, made with pumpkin, mealie meal and water. *One Child, One Seed* (Frances Lincoln in association with Oxfam, March 2002), a counting book for key stage 1 / P1-P3, tells the story of people in this area growing and cooking with pumpkins.

Gisele Wulfsohn/Oxfam

5 Growing rice

These three young women, from the Kou Valley near Bobo Dioulasso in Burkina Faso, are transplanting rice seedlings in the paddy fields near their homes. 1,300 hectares of the broad valley bottom have been turned over to rice-growing. Smallholdings were allotted in equal part to local families and to poor farmers encouraged to migrate from the degraded Sahelian drylands in the north of the country. The families of these women have been here for 30 years, and the women have lived here all their lives. They work in the fields every day except Sunday. They say, 'We're friends and we work together. The work is hard: there's no difficulty in sleeping after a day in the rice [fields]. When you look at the old people together, at home, you can see who still has to work in the fields and who is lucky enough to have children to take over the work.' Their names are Damata, Ramata and Salamata, and they are aged 16, 24 and 16 respectively. They have not been to school at all, as their families have needed them to work. The rice provides a good living. Although they eat some of the rice they grow, the local staple food in this area is boiled millet.

Crispin Hughes/Oxfam

6 Children watering a tree seedling

Children from the Ky Anh district of Vietnam water newly planted tree seedlings in the grounds of their primary school. The children are around seven years old, and live near a tidal river that runs into the South China Sea 50km east of the border with Laos. Trees help give protection from the typhoon winds which can devaste settlements on the South China Sea. The trees planted around the school also help provide shade from the sweltering heat which prevails throughout much of the year, keeping classrooms cool. The boy at the back in the striped shirt is Hoàng Xuan Linh, who featured in *Wake up, World!* (Frances Lincoln in association with Oxfam, 1999).

Jim Holmes/Oxfam

7 Feeding chickens

This photo was taken in El Triunfo, a settlement on the Pacific coast of Guatemala. People displaced by conflict live there in makeshift shelters under plastic roofs. At the time the picture was taken (1999), there were about 308 families there. There are very few opportunities for employment outside the community, so most people rely on subsistence farming to survive. Each family has a couple of acres on which they grow maize and beans. The woman in the picture, Petrona Bernardcuyuch, was given some chickens. The settlement has a school and a clinic among its facilities.

Sean Sprague/Oxfam

8 Packed lunch

Alexis Abala, centre, from Alice Springs, Australia, eats her packed lunch with her best friends at school. Alexis's father is Aboriginal. She features in *Wake up, World!* (See under 6 above). Her best friends, Maddie and Jordan, are with her. Alice Springs is home to a diverse population including 20 per cent Arrente Aboriginees. It lies almost directly in the centre of the vast Australian mainland, and the nearest cities (Darwin on the north coast and Adelaide on the south coast) are each about 1,500 kilometres (932 miles) away. The town used to be very remote and isolated, but the advent of modern technology, along with its airport, has helped connect it to the outside world. Although Alice Springs is very hot in summer, winters are mild, with minimum temperatures at around 4°C. The main industries are tourism and cattle-ranching.

Penny Tweedie/Oxfam

9 Hair styling

This photograph was taken in Burkina Faso. There is a huge variety of hairstyles in West Africa. Friends style each other's hair, sometimes using fine plastic-coated wire, as shown in this photograph. Some styles are fairly easy and quick, but some can take up to two days to complete. This girl lives in a village in Boulgou province in eastern Burkina Faso. Her name is Mariam Saré and she is twelve years old. Mariam's school starts at 7.30, and she has to leave the house at 6.00 in order to get there on time. The first lesson is usually PE.

Crispin Hughes/Oxfam

10 Baking bread

This picture was taken in San Juan de Lurigancho, not far from Lima, Peru, in a bakery set up by local women to make bread initially intended for their own consumption. They now sell the bread. They produce ten types of bread and about eight types of cake. Although they started off with a charcoal-burning oven, they now have a gas oven and other modern equipment, such as a dough kneader and a dough cutter. The bakery and some other projects provide local people with good livelihoods. They used to depend on subsistence agriculture, but were badly affected by El Niño.

Annie Bungeroth/Oxfam

11 Boy in snow

This picture was taken in Lekarstvennoye, Siberia, Russia. The boy, Sasha, aged eight, features in *Wake up, World!* He is carrying a churn of water which he has collected from the well. The Siberian climate is severe, with long winters and short summers. The temperature can drop to -60°C in winter, and snow lies on the ground from September until May. Summers, however, are pleasant and warm, with temperatures reaching 30°C. Sasha's house, behind him in the picture, is made of wood.

Sarah Errington/Oxfam

12 At the bottle bank

This girl, Rosy aged five, lives on the Chicksand Estate in East London, UK. The recycling container she is using is on Spitalfields City Farm near her home. Her family recycles their waste regularly.

Compared to many other countries, the UK is heavily industrialised. England was one of the first countries to become industrialised, and so not many families have close links to the land any more. Agriculture is highly mechanised, and is no longer a major employer. Most people live in towns and cities. One of the challenges facing the UK today is how to dispose of the huge quantities of waste it produces. At the time of writing, only nine per cent of UK household waste is being recycled. Most of it is incinerated or buried in landfill sites, causing pollution and depleting natural resources.

Phil Maxwell

POSTER

Girl pouring water collected from a well into a storage container.

This girl, Mariam, comes from a village in Boulgou province, eastern Burkina Faso. She is aged about 13. Although she attends school, she has to help out a lot with the household chores, both in the evenings and at weekends. N.B. This is not the same Mariam as pictured on Photocard 9.

Crispin Hughes/Oxfam

2 Girl doing the washing up.

This photograph was taken in the UK. The girl, Paige, lives in Brighton. She features in *Wake up, World!* (Frances Lincoln in association with Oxfam, 1999). She is eight years old and has one sister.

Howard Davies

Girl pumping water

This photograph was taken near Piura, northwestern Peru, and shows a young girl using a hand pump. There is a rural development programme there, where people are encouraged to diversify the crops they grow, and become more self-sufficient.

Annie Bungeroth/Oxfam

Man and boys in dug-out canoe

These people are Kampa Indians and are pictured in the Acre province of Brazil, close to the border with Peru. The river they are on is part of the Amazon basin. The Kampa make their living from the forest and the land, and for them, rivers are major highways. Often, the only way to get to the nearest town is by river. They have been given protection by the Brazilian government, which has demarcated their land, making them them less vulnerable to loggers, gold prospectors and commercial farming interests.

Mike Goldwater/Network

Mexican boys playing in water

These boys are jumping from a fishing boat into the sea. The photograph was taken in Celestun, Yucatan, on the Gulf of Mexico. Here, it is used to illustrate how water can be used for recreational purposes.

Edward Parker/Hutchison picture library

Cambodian boy watering garden

This boy is watering the vegetable garden at his school in Kampong Cham Province. Each morning, children water the garden, and the vegetables grown there help supplement the free breakfasts which are given to the children every morning. There are just over 500 pupils at the school, nearly half of them girls. The pupils attend school in two shifts, morning and afternoon. The free meals attract pupils, and absence rates have fallen dramatically since they were introduced – so much so that the school is in danger of becoming overcrowded. The school is partly funded by the government, but it also receives vital funding from NGOs. Part of the money they provide goes towards scholarships which enable families to buy uniforms and equipment so that their children can attend school.

Howard Davies/Oxfam

Unit 1 — Where in the photo?

LEARNING OUTCOMES

► To help children become familiar with the set of photos in this pack

► To develop observation skills

► To introduce some basic science vocabulary and ideas

► To develop further familiarity with the photos

Activity 1.1

Time needed: 30 minutes

YOU WILL NEED

✔ The set of photos from this pack

✔ A copy of worksheet 1 photocopied onto thin card and cut up into separate image cards

Introducing the activity

Display the set of photos around the room so that children can get close to them and observe them carefully. Create 12 small groups of two to three children and give each group one image card. In their groups, they should first of all discuss what they think the image is. Then ask each group to walk round the room and find the photo which contains the image on their card. Having found the image, they should stand next to the photo.

What the children do

Ask each group in turn to point out to the rest of the class which part of the photo their image comes from, and to explain what the image shows. Ask them to describe the photo, saying what they can see and what they think is happening. Allow the class to ask the group and you questions about each photo. Ask each group to leave their image card next to the photo, and invite the whole class to circulate round the room looking at each photo.

Encourage the children to look more closely at the photos by asking questions such as, 'Where do you think this photo was taken?', 'Is it a hot or a cold country?', 'How can you tell?', 'Who do you think the people in the photos are?', 'What are they doing?', 'What questions would you like to ask the people in the photo?'

Another way to do this activity is for the children to be sitting in a circle. Give one photo to each of the 12 groups of two or three children. Hold up one of the image cards and then pass the card round the circle asking them to see if they can match it to their photo. If they cannot they should pass the card on to the next group, and so on.

Introducing science

During this activity, you can start to introduce some basic science vocabulary and ideas.

Hold up some of the photos and ask them what they think they might be able to smell or hear if they were actually 'in the photo'.

Ask them in which photos they can see a pattern (e.g. pattern of leaves, pattern on fabric, rows of loaves, rows of rice plants growing).

Encourage an enquiry approach by posing questions for them such as 'How...?' and 'What would happen if...?'

Teacher's note

It is a good idea to introduce the children to the photos in different contexts and at different times. In this way, they will already be familiar with the photos when you come to focus on a specific learning outcome.

Activity 1.2

Time needed: 30 minutes

YOU WILL NEED
. . . .

✔ The set of photos from the pack

✔ Enlarged copies of worksheet 2 cut up into flashcards

Introducing the activity

Before you start this activity, select the words from the flashcards that are most appropriate for your class. You may wish only to use a few and to explore their meaning in more depth, or to use this activity as a way of introducing a wider range of words. This is a good way to introduce new words to the class that you may wish to use in a later lesson.

Hand round the photos so that each group of two or three children has one photo. Hold up a flashcard and ask what the word on it means. Make sure that the children understand what each word means before continuing.

Ask them to look at their photo and discuss in their group if the word applies to their photo. Most of the words apply to more than one picture so after one group has 'claimed' the word, ask the other groups if it also applies to theirs. They should explain to the class how it applies to their picture.

Further work

Follow on with some or all of these activities:

To explore **opposites** pick out parts of words (light and heavy, light and dark, long and short, wet and dry, hot and cold; for the more able, transparent and opaque). Hand the words out to the groups and ask them to pair up with their opposite. Point out that the word light has two meanings.

To help children start to **classify** words ask them which words are parts of the body, (hands, feet, hair), which are materials (glass, wood, metal, fabric, plastic), which belong to a plant (leaf, seed, wood). This can be done with the children sitting in a circle or more actively by asking them to go and stand in groups with their word card.

To help children think about **processes** ask them to think up sentences with these sets of words in them: bread and bake, eat and food, snow and cold, seed and grow.

eat	grow	water
light	wood	glass
metal	plants	hands
cold	seed	feet
leaf	shadow	food
bread	hot	reflection
wet	sun	sky
animal	snow	clothes
dark	move	dry
bake	tree	sound
long	short	shade
heavy	fabric	plastic

These words are more difficult but you may be able to use them with some of the children.

reflection	weight	braiding
protection	recycling	balance
load	hygiene	waste
opaque	inanimate	living

Me and my shadow

LEARNING OUTCOMES

▶ Identify the sun as a source of light

▶ Learn how shadows are caused

▶ Learn that shadows change shape and size with the movement of the sun

▶ Learn that shadows can indicate the time of day

Activity 2.1

Time needed: 1 hour

YOU WILL NEED

✔ Photograph 1: shadows

✔ Enough chalk sticks for one between two

✔ A sunny day

✔ The other photos in the pack (for extension work)

Introducing the activity

Display the photograph so that all the children can see it. Ask them what they can see in the photo. Ask them some general questions about the photo such as 'Was it taken in a hot or cold place?' and 'How can you tell?' (The sun is obviously shining and the people have no shoes on.) Explain to the children that you are going to investigate shadows, what causes them and what happens to them during the day.

What the children do

Take the children outside and ask them to stand in a line shoulder to shoulder with the sun behind them. Ask them to point to where their shadow is. Show them that they are all pointing in the same direction. Now ask them to turn to the left so that they are all facing the same direction. Ask them what has happened to their shadow. Then ask them, working in pairs, to draw around each other's shadow and to draw a circle where they were standing. Make sure each child knows which is their circle. (They could write their name in it.) Return at least an hour later. Ask the children to stand in their original spots. What has happened to their shadow?

Plenary

Back in the classroom, explain that their bodies were blocking the light and that this is what caused a shadow. Opaque objects, such as their bodies, wood, stone, metal etc. do not allow light to pass through them. If you are able to darken the classroom, you may want to demonstrate this with a torch and a book to help the children understand. Show how, the lower the source of light, the longer the shadow is. Explain that the sun is at its highest at midday. Now look at the photo again and ask them if they can tell what time of day it was when it was taken.

Activity 2.2

Time needed: 30 minutes

YOU WILL NEED
. . . .

✔ The complete set of photos from the pack

Introducing the activity

Remind the children that when the source of light is low, the shadow is long.

What the children do

Pass round the other photos from the pack. As they look at the photos the children should note whether there is a shadow in the photo or not. Ask them to pick out those with shadows, and display these where all the children can see them. (Make sure you have the photos of the boy in the snow and the boy with the donkey.)

Plenary

Ask them why there are no shadows in some of the photos. Now look at the photos on display. What do they notice about the shadows in both the photos? (They are long, meaning that the sun is low in the sky.) You may wish to introduce the idea that in countries near the equator the sun is overhead at midday – nearer the poles it stays low in the sky and produces long shadows. Ask the children for the names of some hot countries (where shadows are shorter) and cold countries (where shadows are longer). You could use the world map on the back of the poster for this.

Further work

Some pupils might like to investigate the history of sundials and how they work.

For 'homework', pupils could be asked to look at shadows around where they live. They should choose an object, such as a tree or a lamp post, and observe its shadow at different times of the day.

Wordbank

shadow

shade

opaque

transparent

cooler

warmer

longer

shorter

Unit 3 — Drumming

LEARNING OUTCOMES

▶ Explore the ways that sound is made by musical instruments

▶ Understand that sound is caused by vibrations

Activity 3

Time needed: 1 hour

YOU WILL NEED

✔ Photograph 2: girl with drum

✔ Recording of some African drumming (can be downloaded from: www.oxfam.org.uk/coolplanet/teachers)

✔ A drum (two drums of different sizes would be useful)

✔ A variety of plastic basins/bowls, margarine tubs and yoghurt pots

✔ Thin plastic bags, greaseproof paper and aluminium foil

✔ Sticky tape

✔ Elastic bands

✔ Rice

✔ Optional: a selection of musical instruments, from different countries if possible

Introducing the activity

Show the children the photograph and explain that this girl lives in Mozambique. Point to Mozambique on a world map to show where it is. What is the girl doing? Play a recording of some African drumming.

Ask the children which musical instruments they have played, and whether they know how the sound is made in each case. Collect a list of ideas and record them on the blackboard – they will probably include banging, plucking, shaking or blowing. Demonstrate with instruments. Bang the drum again and ask how the sound is made. Scatter rice on the drum to demonstrate vibration. For a sound to be produced there must be some kind of movement or vibration. Which parts of the drum vibrate?

Teacher's note: It is the skin on the drum which vibrates to make a sound. This in turn causes the air to vibrate, which causes our eardrums to vibrate and we hear the sound.

Ask the children to predict what would happen if we stopped the vibrations. Hit the drum and then place a hand on the skin to stop the movement.

What the children do

Ask the children how they think they could make their own drum. Put the materials on a table and invite the children to look at what is available. Ask them to discuss in small groups how they could make a drum. Check that their ideas are feasible and ask them to go ahead. When they have made their drums, they can put some rice on the 'skin' and observe what happens when they bang the drum. When they have finished, they can make other instruments by stretching elastic bands across pots. Get the children to draw a picture of their drum and to write about how the sound is produced.

Plenary

Compare the sounds made by the different drums they have produced. Ask them to give their ideas as to why the sounds are different. How is the sound affected by the size of the drum, or the materials of which it is made? What happens if the skin is not tight? Why do they think this makes a difference? Ask them how the sound is produced from the pots with the elastic bands.

Further work

Demonstrate a variety of instruments and let the children discuss how the sounds are made in each case. Ask the children to make a quiet sound rather than a loud sound with some of the instruments.

Listen to recordings of music from different cultures, particularly those which feature one instrument. CD ROMs are good for this as they often give background information and pictures.

Wordbank		
vibration	sound	quiet
movement	loud	listen
hear		

Unit 4 Balancing the load

LEARNING OUTCOMES

▶ Learn how to carry out an investigation

▶ Understand that forces can balance each other

Activity 4

Time needed: 45 minutes

YOU WILL NEED

✔ Photograph 3: boy with donkey

✔ About 20 carrier bags

✔ A selection of bags such as rucksacks, shoulder bags, etc

✔ Books

✔ Optional: several photos from a range of countries showing people carrying things in different ways

Introducing the activity

Important note: Teachers should ensure that children do not carry too many books at once.

Put as many books as possible into a carrier bag and ask several children to lift it and comment on whether it is heavy or not. Ask them how they could carry the books more easily. Put half the books into a second bag and now ask them to lift the two bags. Is it easier to carry the load this way? Now show them the photo, pointing out that the donkey is carrying a heavy load of nuts. The load is balanced so the weight is spread out more. Ask them what would happen if all the nuts were on one side only.

What the children do

Ask the children to work in groups of three or four. Tell them they are going to investigate the easiest way to carry heavy loads. Give them a pile of books each, and ask them to think of some of the tests they could make up to find this out. Give them two carrier bags and a few other bags. They might consider putting the loads on different parts of their body, for example heads, shoulders or back, and distributing the weight evenly. They should record their findings.

Plenary

Bring the children together to share their findings and discuss what they did to reach their conclusions. Discuss how they could display what they have discovered. Show the children a selection of photos (if available), including ones from a range of different countries, of people carrying things in different ways; for example women carrying buckets or bowls of water on their heads, or children carrying firewood.

Wordbank
load
heavy
balance
easy
easier
easiest

LEARNING OUTCOMES

▶ Discover that fruits contain seeds and that these grow into plants

▶ Observe the different patterns and quantities of seeds in fruits

▶ Think about seed dispersal

Activity 5

Time needed: An hour and a half. The activity will take less time if the close observational drawing is omitted.

YOU WILL NEED

✔ Photograph 4: slicing a pumpkin

✔ Worksheet 3

✔ Fruits and vegetables containing seeds, including pumpkin if it is in season

Teacher's note

This unit is on the same theme as 'Growing rice' (Unit 6).

Introducing the activity

Show the children the photograph and ask them for their ideas about it. What do they think the person is doing with the pumpkin? What can they see in the middle? What do they think the person is going to do with the seeds? Tell the children that she will probably save some of them, in order to grow more pumpkins.

Ask the children if they have ever eaten pumpkin, or if they ever have ever seen one. It is likely that many children will have seen a pumpkin at Hallowe'en when they are made into lanterns, but they may not have eaten it as a vegetable. Tell the children that a lot of people eat pumpkin as a vegetable, especially in parts of Africa and in the Caribbean; and that Americans eat pumpkin pie for Thanksgiving, a special celebration which takes place in November every year. This photograph of a pumpkin was taken in KwaZulu Natal, South Africa, where pumpkin forms a large part of people's diet. See Photo information for teachers (page 7) for more details.

What the children do

Divide the children into groups, and give each group a small selection of fruits and vegetables which contain seeds, such as apples, pears, plums, pumpkin, tomatoes and also some fruits less familiar to the children. Ask them to predict which fruits will have a lot of seeds inside and which will have just a few, what colour the seeds are likely to be, and whether they will be large or small. Cut the fruits open one at a time so that the children can look closely at the seeds.

Give the children magnifiers and tell them to make a close observational drawing of one of the fruits or vegetables. They could use colour if wished.

Tell the children to take the seeds out and count them. If there are more than ten, they should put them into piles of ten.

They should record their results; worksheet 3 could be used for this.

Plenary

Get the children to report back their findings about which fruits and vegetables had the most or fewest seeds. Talk about where the seeds are in the fruit, and the pattern they make. Ask the children to think about why some plants produce so many seeds. Do they think they will all grow? How do the seeds 'get away from the plant?' Briefly discuss the way seeds are dispersed: wind, animals, falling on the ground. In what conditions will they grow? (There is more on this in the next unit.)

Further work

Prepare a display showing fruits and vegetables, including some less common ones. Try to collect names in different community languages (if applicable) and display these next to the fruits and vegetables. Often, names vary according to country, not just language. The children could ask their parents for names of the vegetables they eat at home.

Wordbank

germinate	pumpkin
grow	fruit
seed	vegetable

Worksheet 3 | Seeds and fruits

What I think I will find

Fruit	Number of seeds	Size of seeds	Colour of seeds

What I found

Fruit	Number of seeds	Size of seeds	Colour of seeds

LEARNING OUTCOMES

▶ Learn that plants are living and that they grow

▶ Learn that plants need water and light to grow

▶ Discover that seeds grow into plants

▶ Learn that rice is the seed of the rice plant

▶ Learn that some of our food consists of seeds

Activity 6

Time needed: 1 hour, and then 10 minutes every few days to look at their seeds and to talk about their progress.

YOU WILL NEED

✔ Photograph 5: growing rice

✔ A packet of wholegrain rice (and samples of other types of rice)

✔ Containers, e.g. small yoghurt pots

✔ Cotton wool or paper towels

✔ Magnifiers

✔ Worksheet 4

Introducing the activity

Show the children a bag (or bags) of wholegrain rice. Give each group a small amount of rice and ask them to look closely at it using a magnifier. (Tell the children not to taste any of the rice.) Ask them where they think rice comes from. If they say a shop, keep asking where the shop gets rice from until you get to the fact that it is the seed of a plant.

Ask the children if they have any ideas about how and where rice grows.

Show the photograph to the children and ask them what the people in it are doing. (They are thinning out the rice seedlings.) You could also ask them what questions they have about the picture, especially if they are unfamiliar with it. See if others in the group can suggest answers to the questions. Start by asking a question yourself,

e.g. 'Do you think the picture shows a hot or a cold country?' Finally, ask the children if they can tell from the photo what rice needs in order to grow.

What the children do

Encourage the children to think how they might try to grow the rice, and show them the equipment which is available (cotton wool, paper towels, yoghurt pots).

Get each group to draw a plan to show how they are going to plant their seeds and how they will look after them.

Teacher's note

Only wholegrain rice will grow. It germinates quite quickly and can easily be grown on damp kitchen paper or cotton wool.

Use worksheet 4 for children's ideas about how they will plant their rice.

Plenary

Ask the children to talk about where rice comes from and how it is grown. Ask each group to report back on their ideas for growing rice, and have regular sessions for reporting back news about how the rice seeds are growing. Ask the children to talk about rice dishes which they enjoy eating.

Wordbank
rice
seedling
grow
flooded
field

Worksheet 4 | Growing rice

I will need: _____

_____

_____

_____

First, I will _____

_____

_____

_____

Next, I will _____

_____

_____

_____

Then, I'll _____

_____

_____

_____

I'm going to remember to _____

_____

_____

_____

Unit 7   A tree is for life

LEARNING OUTCOMES

► Learn that plants need light and water to grow

► Realise why it is important to care for the environment

► Learn the various uses of wood and how these are chosen for specific purposes on the basis of their simple properties

Activity 7.1

Time needed: 45 minutes

YOU WILL NEED

✔ Photograph 6: children watering a tree seedling

✔ Two sheets of sugar paper stuck together on which you have drawn the large outline of a tree

✔ Paper from which to cut out leaf shapes

✔ Scissors

✔ Glue

✔ Optional: a range of pictures of things made from wood including houses (see photo 11), people collecting or using wood for fuel, and toys and artefacts from around the world – you can find these in holiday brochures (e.g. Scandinavia, Japan, Madagascar and Borneo), on the internet and in educational photopacks.

Introducing the activity

Show the children the photo and ask them what they can see. Point out to them, if you need to, that the children in the picture are watering a young tree. Ask them why caring for it is important and what would happen if it did not rain and no one watered it. Ask them to talk about other plants they have looked after and what they have had to do to care for them (watering, weeding, feeding, pruning). What would happen if trees did not exist? Who else depends on trees? (Birds and animals for food and homes.) What about humans? Why do we need trees? If the children have difficulty, point

out that wood comes from trees.

What the children do

In pairs, the children should draw a large leaf on a piece of paper and cut it out so that they have a leaf-shaped piece of paper. They should then go round the room and identify everything they can find made from wood (chairs, desks, doors, windows, pencils, floor etc.). They should write or draw these onto the leaf-shaped pieces of paper and stick them onto the branches of the tree on the sheet of sugar paper.

Plenary

Look at the display and ask the children to think of other uses of wood. Point out to them that other uses include houses, firewood, works of art and toys. If you have pictures showing the uses of wood in other parts of the world, pass them round, asking the children to notice how the wood has been used and emphasising how useful wood is to us. Point out that we have to buy wood from other countries as we don't grow enough trees in the UK. Ask the children if they can think of any problems with using wood to make lots of things (use up the trees). Summarise the main ideas about why trees are important. Get the children to share ideas about how we can look after trees. Ask the class to think of as many things as they can that they have learnt about trees. If they run out of ideas to share, they could think of questions instead.

Activity 7.2

Time needed: 1 hour

YOU WILL NEED

✔ Dry weather

✔ A tree

Introducing the activity

Tell the children you are going to go out to look at a tree. Ask them what they already know about trees. What would they like to know about trees? Tell them they are going to go out and look closely at a tree.

What the children do

Take the children out to look at a large tree. When you get to the tree, measure the spread of the branches. How many strides does it take to go from one side to the other across the shadow? Can everybody fit under the tree? Get a few children to join hands around the trunk to find out how large the trunk is. Depending on the time of the year, look at the leaves and look for fruits or seeds. Ask the children for their ideas about creatures which may live there. Get the children to stand back from the tree and get them to look at the base of the tree trunk. Get them to look at the colour of the trunk, the way it divides into branches, and the what shape the leaves are. It might be possible to find some insects on the trunk.

Back in the classroom, the children should draw the tree, in colour if wished, and write what they found out about it.

Plenary

Children can share the information they have collected about the tree. You can continue the discussion about what they would like to know about trees, answering their questions and helping them to think where they could find the information. Widen the discussion to talk about trees in other countries. What trees do they know of which do not grow in the UK? What are those trees like?

Wordbank

tree

trunk

branch

air

roots

shade

creatures

The animal world

LEARNING OUTCOMES

. . . .

► Learn that we need to take care of some living things, while some can take care of themselves

► Know that all living things need food and water

► Learn that living things can be classified into different types

Activity 8

Time needed: 1 hour

YOU WILL NEED

. . . .

✔ Photograph 7: feeding chickens

✔ Worksheet 5 – enough copies for one between two

✔ Worksheet 6 – enough for one each

Introducing the activity

Show the children the photo. Ask them what is happening. Ask them why they think the woman is keeping hens, and briefly talk to them about how we often depend on animals not just for food but other things as well. Ask them where wool, leather and milk come from. Explain that animals that are specially bred need to be looked after. If they have pets, they could talk about how they look after them.

Ask the children to work in pairs. They should cut up worksheet 5 into squares, each showing a picture of an animal. Ask them to sort the animal cards into groups. You could accept any reasonable groupings.

Now ask them if they can sort the cards into these three groups:

• pets

• farm animals / animals for food / working animals

• wild animals.

Individually, each child should now fill in worksheet 6 showing what animals eat and drink. Ask them to think about the difference between

how pets and farm animals on the one hand, and wild animals on the other get their food, and to compare their ideas with a friend.

Plenary

Ask the children to share their ideas about what they have learnt. Make sure they have understood:

• What animals need for their physical survival (food and water)

• What some animals eat

• How we can classify animals in different ways (wild, tame and working animals etc).

Further work

Children could leave wild birdseed out (in winter only) and observe which birds come and eat it. The teacher could put a list of these birds on the wall, adding pictures, if available.

Children could devise instructions for someone who was going to look after their pet while they went on holiday.

Children could find out where some of the animals on worksheet 5 come from. It may not be feasible for them to name specific countries, but they could name continents, or at least climates/habitats, e.g. hot countries or cold countries, jungles, forests, deserts, sea etc.

Wordbank
animal
feed
food
farm
human
tame
wild
bird

Worksheet 6 What animals eat

eats →

eats →

eats →

eats →

eats →

Unit 9 — What's in my lunch box?

LEARNING OUTCOMES

► Learn that humans need food and water to stay alive

► Learn that eating the right type and amount of food help humans to keep healthy

► Learn to group things according to observable similarities and differences

Activity 9.1

Time needed: 1 hour

YOU WILL NEED

✔ Photograph 8: packed lunch

✔ Worksheet 7

Introducing the activity

Display the photo where all the children can see it. Discuss with the children what they can see and where they think the photograph was taken. How can they tell? Explain that it is in Australia and it shows children eating their packed lunch. Do any of the children in the class bring a packed lunch with them? What do they have in their packed lunch? Ask them to talk in pairs about what they have had, or are having for lunch, then ask the class for some of the foods they have mentioned, and list them on the board. Go through the list, and discuss with the class whether it is possible to sort these foods into different groups. Make lists of these groups on the board. If you feel it is appropriate, explain to the children that a balanced meal usually contains foods from these groups: energy-giving foods (bread, potatoes, pasta, rice, pastry), fruit and vegetables, and protein (nuts, meat, fish, beans or lentils, cheese and other dairy products). Explain that all humans need a variety of foods to stay healthy – but not too much of some foods.

What the children do

Give the children worksheet 7, and ask them to draw a healthy lunch and a not so healthy lunch.

Plenary

The children should share with the others what they would put in their lunch box. What were the similarities and differences? What have they found out about healthy eating? Is it important to have a range of food? Take one of the not so healthy lunches as an example, and ask the children how they would feel after they had eaten it? What effect would it have on their teeth?

Fill the lunchboxes

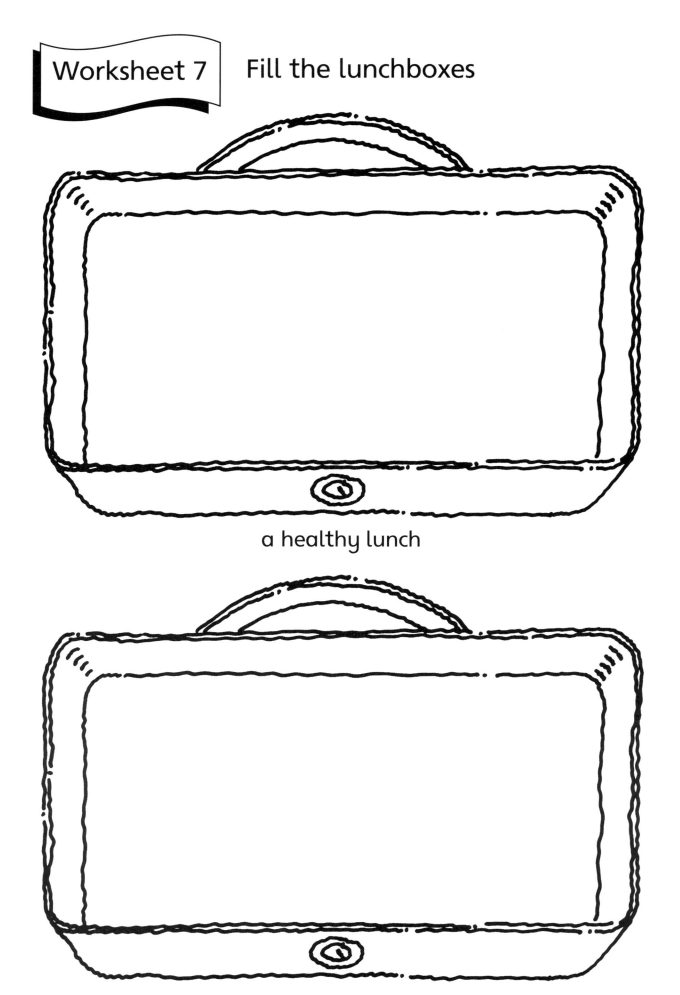

a healthy lunch

a not so healthy lunch

Activity 9.2

Time needed: 1 hour

YOU WILL NEED

· ·

✔ Loaf (or 2) of sliced bread

✔ Jam

✔ Fridge

✔ Aluminium foil

✔ Greaseproof paper

Introducing the activity

Remind the children about the need to eat a healthy diet. Tell them it is also important that food is fresh. Ask them how we keep food fresh in this country. When they say 'fridge' ask them if everyone in the world has a fridge. Show them the photo again, pass it round the group and ask how the children have kept their lunch fresh (there is foil covering the sandwiches). Tell the children they are going to do an 'investigation' to find out which keeps sandwiches freshest: aluminium foil, greaseproof paper or no wrapping at all; in the fridge or out of the fridge? Ask them to predict which will be the freshest in a few hours time.

What the children do

Each group of three or four children should make six jam sandwiches (using six slices of bread – three rounds cut in half). They should wrap two sandwiches in greaseproof paper, two in aluminium foil and leave two unwrapped. They should put one of each into the fridge and leave the other out.

After a couple of hours, ask the children to think how they can test how fresh the sandwiches are, without eating them (smell, touch, sight). Record the findings using a Carroll diagram (see opposite).

Plenary

The children report back on their findings to the rest of the class. How can they can keep food fresh? Which foods go bad most quickly? What did people in the UK do before fridges were invented? Talk about how people in hot countries keep their food fresh. What do they do if they have not got a fridge? (Keep it in a cool shaded room, use dried and salted food, etc.)

Further work

Pupils could follow up the theme of fresh food around the world.

Design and make posters promoting healthy eating.

Wordbank

food

drink

hungry

thirsty

healthy

	wrapped in foil	wrapped in greaseproof paper	unwrapped
How do they smell?			
How do they feel?			
How do they look?			

LEARNING OUTCOMES

▶ Understand what is needed to keep hair healthy

▶ Recognise that there are differences in the type and texture of people's hair but that all human beings also have similarities

Activity 10

Time needed: 1 hour

YOU WILL NEED

✔ Photograph 9: hair styling

✔ Worksheet 8

✔ Coloured pencils

✔ Class set of plastic mirrors

Introducing the activity

Display the photograph and ask the children what is happening. Explain that it shows Mariam, a 12-year-old girl in Burkina Faso, having her hair braided by a friend. This can take several hours but once done it can stay for weeks. In some cases, girls would not be allowed in school if they had not braided their hair. Ask the children what they have to do to their hair to get ready for school.

What the children do

Ask each child to complete worksheet 9, 'How I look after my hair'. They should draw a picture of themselves (head only) in the middle, and then add captions saying how they look after their hair, and who helps them (if applicable). Ask them to tell a partner what they are going to write or draw before they start. To encourage accuracy, provide individual plastic mirrors and ask the children to try and get the skin and hair colours as close as possible.

Plenary

Some children could describe how they look after their hair, and answer questions. Do they look after their hair in a different way from their parents? Does anyone help them? Summarise ideas about how we keep our hair clean and healthy. Some children may use oil on their hair for instance. Talk about the way hair is viewed in different cultures. (Muslim and Jewish women may keep their hair covered, Sikh men do not cut their hair and wear it in turbans, for example.) Emphasise the fact that, although there are physical and cultural differences between human beings, there are also many similarities. Ask them to think of some of these.

Further work

The children could practise plaiting. They should use three strands of wool, ribbon or paper, tie a knot and anchor it at one end.

Wordbank
hair
plait
braid
wash
shampoo
dry

Worksheet 8 | How I look after my hair

1

2

3

4

Name _____

Unit 11 | Baking bread

LEARNING OUTCOMES

▶ Discover that once bread is baked, we cannot change it back into dough (irreversible change)

▶ Describe the way some materials change when they are heated

▶ Learn that dough needs to be baked to turn it into bread

▶ See that there are many different types of bread

▶ Explore bread as an important part of many people's diet

▶ Find out about some of the different types of bread, their names and origins

Activity 11.1

Time needed: 1 hour (for chapattis) or 45 minutes (for toast)

YOU WILL NEED

✔ Photograph 10: baking bread

✔ Ingredients and utensils for chapattis (see recipe, page 35) or bread for toasting

✔ A cooker or toaster

✔ Worksheet 9

Introducing the activity

Make sure that all the children can see the photograph and ask them what is happening. Do they think that this person is baking for a family? Ask the children about where they get their bread. Have they ever seen bread being baked?

Ask the children if they have ever seen or touched dough. What is it like? Ask them what they think happens to the dough when it is in the oven. What changes happen in the way it looks, smells and feels? Which types of bread do they like best, and why?

What the children do

If possible, let groups of children bake some bread, following a simple recipe. Chapattis are relatively simple to cook, especially if you can draw on a parent or helper to demonstrate, and to work with groups. A recipe for chapattis is given on page 35.

If it is not possible to bake bread, the children could make toast so they can see that this change is also irreversible.

Plenary

Talk to the children about how the dough changed into bread, or how the bread changed into toast. Summarise ideas about what happened (bread rose, chapattis became less sticky, toasted bread became crisper).

Ask the children whether you can get the chapattis to change back into dough or the toast to change back into bread. Ask them if they can think of something which they could change back after they had heated or cooked it. (Water would be one example.)

The children can record the activities they tried using a storyboard (worksheet 9). This helps them to report the activity in a chronological sequence.

This is what I did

1

_____

_____

_____

_____

2

_____

_____

_____

_____

3

_____

_____

_____

_____

4

_____

_____

_____

_____

Activity 11.2

Time needed: 45 minutes

YOU WILL NEED

. . . .

✔ Selection of breads such as ciabatta, chapatti, pitta, sliced loaf, cholla, French stick

✔ Margarine or butter

✔ Blunt knives

Introducing the activity

Show the children the photograph. Ask them whether they think bread is popular in the place where this woman lives. Ask them how much bread they eat and how often they eat it. Ask them what type of food they eat most of. Make a list on the board. Explain to them that people in many other countries eat very different food, and that, when we would eat bread at a meal, they might eat rice, noodles, porridge or something else filling.

Tell them that bread is eaten in many different countries around the world, and that it comes in all sorts of shapes and sizes. Ask the children what types of bread they have eaten and whether they know the names of the types of bread. Show them the breads you have brought in, and tell them the names and the countries of origin.

What the children do

Divide the children into groups of about four. Give each group part of a loaf of bread. Get the children to compare breads – they could sort them into two groups, or devise their own groupings such as ones they have eaten, ones they haven't, good for making sandwiches, good for dipping into things etc. Cut small pieces of the bread for the children to try, perhaps with some margarine or butter (be aware of hygiene and dietary requirements).

Plenary

Ask the children to share their ideas about how they grouped their bread samples. Which new breads have they tried, which of these did they like best and why?

Further work

Make a display showing different types of bread. Label the breads and say which countries they originally came from. You could use a map to show this, perhaps linking the bread with string or wool to its country or origin. Encourage the children to bring in other types of bread and to write the name of the bread in their home language (where applicable). Most supermarkets now stock a very wide variety of breads of different origins.

Some children may be able to explain how they eat special breads for festivals or religious occasions.

More work could be done on food from around the world. Food in general is often the subject of special festivals, e.g. the Yam Festival in Nigeria.

Wordbank

names of breads

oven

heat

bake

dough

rises

changes

yeast

Recipe for chapattis

Ingredients

- ✔ 175g chapatti flour (or wholegrain flour, if unavailable)
- ✔ 1/2 teaspoon salt
- ✔ water
- ✔ vegetable oil
- ✔ more flour for dusting

Sift the flour and salt into a large mixing bowl. Make a well in the centre of the flour and then add the water gradually to make a smooth dough which isn't too wet.

Knead the dough until soft and pliable.

Divide it into six portions shaped into balls. Keep the dough you are not using covered.

Dust the rolling pin and each ball of dough in flour. Roll a ball of dough out on a floured surface to make a circle approximately 17cm in diameter.

Heat some oil in a heavy frying pan. When it is hot, fry the chapatti dough on both sides until browned, pressing the edges down with a spoon as it cooks.

Brush one side of each of the cooked chapattis with a little melted butter and keep it warm while you cook the remainder. Serve warm.

Unit 12 Keeping warm

LEARNING OUTCOMES

► Introduce the children to the idea of insulation

► Recognise materials which are good insulators

► Explore the idea that winter clothing consists of more layers and different fabrics to summer clothing

► Explore how long it takes things to cool down to the temperature of their surroundings

► Find out about the uses of a variety of materials and how these are chosen for specific purposes

Activity 12.1

Time needed: 1 hour

YOU WILL NEED

✔ Photograph 11: boy in snow

✔ Samples of different fabrics including thick and thin, natural and man-made

Introducing the activity

Show the children the photo and ask them to think of some questions about it. Discuss their questions and answers. Ask them what time of the year they think it is? What kind of clothes is the boy wearing?

Ask the children to describe what they were wearing today when they came to school and how this would be different in summer/winter.

Hold up some pieces of fabric and ask the children to say whether each one would be useful for summer clothes or winter clothes. You will probably need to introduce the idea of layers, and say that in winter we may wear some clothes such as underclothes or shirts and blouses made of thin fabrics but we would include more layers of clothing on top of these. Although there is no need to go into detail on this point, you can tell the children that several layers of thinner fabric are sometimes warmer than one layer of thicker fabric because of the air trapped in between.

What the children do

Give each group a selection of different fabrics and ask them to decide which ones they would choose for going to the park on a winter day. They have to have three layers – which one would they have next to their skin, and which would be next, and which would they have on the outside? Tell them to think of reasons for their choices.

Ask them to think about why the outside layer might need to be different from the clothing next to their bodies, and encourage them to think about rain, snow and wind.

Plenary

Ask the children to talk about their ideas.

Activity 12.2

YOU WILL NEED

- ✔ Photograph 11: boy in snow
- ✔ Small plastic bottles with lids
- ✔ Containers from which to fill them (eg jugs)
- ✔ Funnels
- ✔ Samples of different fabrics including thick and thin, natural and man-made
- ✔ Elastic bands
- ✔ Optional: thermometers or heat sensors to be linked to computers

Introducing the activity

Tell the children that they are going to set up a test to find out which keeps something warmer longer, three layers or one layer.

What the children do

Divide the children into groups and give each group two empty bottles. They should choose layers of fabric, cut them to fit the bottles (if necessary) and practise wrapping them around them. They should wrap one bottle with one layer of fabric and the other with three layers of fabric, and then secure the fabric with elastic bands. The teacher should than fill the bottles with hot water using a funnel. Ask the children to think about how they will find out which bottle of water cools down the most / the quickest.

In order to measure the temperature of the water, they could use a thermometer, although the scales are quite difficult for children to read, or you could use a heat sensor which links to a computer. These make reading the scales quite easy and everyone can see it at the same time. Alternatively, the children can feel the bottles and judge which bottle of water has cooled down more.

Get the children to record their investigation.

Plenary

Summarise the children's findings about keeping things warm. Get each group to report back on their investigation, saying how effective layers are as a way of keeping warm.

Further work

Discuss with the children what kind of clothes and fabrics are suitable for wearing in hot countries and what is suitable for cold countries. You could talk about why it is good to keep the sun off your head, and what type of clothes are suitable for this (hats, headscarves, etc.). You could look at the different types of headwear and footwear which are suitable for different climates. Some of the other photos in the pack could be used in these discussions.

Wordbank

warm, warmer, warmest

layers

fabric

cool, cooler coolest

bottle

water

funnel

Unit 13 Recycling

LEARNING OUTCOMES

▶ Sort items according to the material from which they are made

▶ Learn that some materials can be recycled

▶ Investigate litter in the locality and think about how we can take care of the environment

▶ Begin to understand that the earth's resources are finite and to learn about the importance of recycling

Activity 13

Time needed: 1 hour

YOU WILL NEED

✔ Photograph 12: at the bottle bank

✔ Selection of objects made from different materials

✔ Bin bags

✔ Clipboards

✔ plastic or rubber gloves

Introducing the activity

Make sure that all the children can see the photograph. Ask them what they think it is showing. What is the girl doing? Why is she putting the bottle through the hole?

Ask the children what is going to happen to the bottle. Summarise their ideas, then tell them that the glass will be melted down and made into new things. Get the children to list all the things they (and their family) might throw into a waste bin at home.

Ask them what happens to all the things which they throw away at home. What do they think happens to litter which is thrown onto the ground?

What the children do

Get the children to carry out a litter survey around the school. Firstly, ask them to predict what they might find. What different types of materials can they find?

Ask the children what they think will happen if they leave some of the litter on the ground – for example a piece of apple, some paper and a can – and at the same time bury some of the same things in the earth. Leave both groups of rubbish for one week and then see what happens to them. Children should only touch the litter if they are wearing plastic gloves.

Plenary

Discuss the photograph again, explaining in more detail what happens to materials which are recycled. Show children some containers which have a recycling sign on them (a looped arrow). Discuss the importance of taking waste materials to the recycling skips, or of sorting our refuse, if this option is available.

Summarise main ideas about what happens to:

• rubbish from home

• rubbish which people throw onto the ground

• rubbish which is put into recycling banks.

Talk to the children about why recycling helps us to look after the environment. Explain to them that it helps us to save raw materials (such as sand, trees and metals) and energy. Ask the children how we can look after the environment.

Further work

Children could summarise their ideas on a poster or in a concertina book.

Wordbank

materials

glass

metal

recycle

rubbish

litter

Using the A1 poster

The A1 poster is suitable for general classroom display, for whole class and/or group work, and as a starting point for other work. The poster can be displayed on a flip chart or whiteboard with the class gathered round for discussion work.

Some ideas for using the poster are listed below.

GENERAL DISCUSSION: USES OF WATER

Start by brainstorming with the children all the different ways they use water. What would it be like if we didn't have water? Ask them where water comes from. Display the photo to the children and ask them to tell you the different ways in which people on the poster are using water (for playing, keeping cool, helping plants grow, travelling on and washing dishes). Ask them what uses for water aren't shown on the poster (drinking, washing ourselves, fish breathe in it). Make it clear to the children that water has many uses and that all human beings, animals and plants need water to survive.

Where does water come from? Look at the pictures on the poster and ask the children where people get their water from. Point out the little girl doing the washing up, the girl with the bowl of water on her head and the girl at the water pump.

PRACTICAL ACTIVITY: WEIGHT OF WATER

You will need a bucket approximately the size of the bucket in the photo of the girl at the water pump. You will also need enough 500cl plastic bottles to almost fill the bucket, such as the ones bottled water is sold in. Fill these with water from the tap.

Ask the children to look at the bucket and to imagine how heavy it would be if it were full of water. Would they be able to carry it? Do they think the girl in the photo carries the bucket full of water? Take the bottles of water and bucket to the playground and fill the bucket one bottle at a time. After every litre or so ask one of the children to carry the bucket a measured distance. They should make a note of how much water is going in the bucket and at what point it becomes too heavy to carry the distance. Return to the classroom and remind them that the girl in the photo probably carries the bucket full of water at least a few hundred metres every day and that it is common in many countries for girls to collect water like this. Also look at the boy watering plants. Ask the children how he is able to carry two heavy watering cans. Compare this with the photo in the pack of the donkey carrying the balanced baskets.

USING THE WORLD MAP

The large world map on the reverse of the A1 poster can be used to support work in a number of areas, including geography. All the countries featured in the photocards and on the A1 poster are labelled on the map.

Ask the children for suggestions about how you could travel from the UK to one other country. Develop the ideas into a route plan and list all the countries you would travel through (or over) on the way.

Children will enjoy choosing a stage of the journey and drawing the form of transport they would use. Help children get a sense of distance by explaining how long it would take to get somewhere overland and by air. Encourage children to talk about a long journey they have made themselves. Encourage the children to use appropriate geographical vocabulary such as north and south, to think about how climates vary around the world, and point out the time differences between the countries.

Resources

SCIENCE AND OTHER USEFUL RESOURCES

Most of the resources below can be ordered from Oxfam's catalogue, *Oxfam Education Resources for Schools 2001–2002*. The catalogue is available free. For a copy, please phone Supporter Services on 01865 312610, or e-mail: oxfam@oxfam.org.uk

The catalogue has details of many other topic-based photopacks for use in the primary classroom. Use the comprehensive index to find photopacks on topics such as agriculture, children, cities, the environment, food, journeys, transport and water. The catalogue also has many photo-based resources which focus on specific places around the world.

A World of Investigations
A colour photopack (aimed at key stages 1 and 2) which offers practical activities for using photographs to encourage an investigative approach to science. It shows how photos can help children develop skills in generating questions, planning investigations, and evaluating the outcomes.
Birmingham DEC, 1996 (To order, phone 0121 472 3255)

Toying with Technology
This resource, designed to bring a global perspective to work on toys and technology, includes a photopack, video, storybook and A3 map of Africa. It shows how Kondi, a boy from Malawi, makes his own car from scrap wire. Pupils are then encouraged to make their own simple toys from everyday materials.
Scottish DEC/Oxfam, 2000

Making a Difference
A resource for Key Stage 2 which brings sustainable development to life. It contains a range of stimulating activities which encourage children to think about how they can be actively involved in making a difference. Themes include recycling, water, electricity and fair trade. Useful for PSHE, citizenship and PSD. Bilingual – English and Welsh. Available free of charge to schools in Wales.
Oxfam/RSPB, 2001

Making it Happen: Agenda 21 and Schools
Aimed at pupils aged seven to eleven, this book provides a background to the importance of Agenda 21, and focuses on ways schools can engage with the process at a local level. It offers a variety of case studies, activity ideas and approaches to explore environment, citizenship and sustainability across the curriculum.
WWF-UK, 1998

One Child, One Seed
Kathryn Cave
This counting book for young children is set in a remote rural community in KwaZulu Natal, South Africa, which is where the photo for unit 5, Fruits and seeds, was taken. It tells the story of Nothando, a young girl who plants a pumpkin seed and watches it grow. It shows how pumpkin is a staple food in this area, and intro-duces information about how things grow, how to take care of them and daily life in an agricultural community.
Frances Lincoln, in association with Oxfam GB. Available March 2002.

Wake Up, World!
Beatrice Hollyer
Join children and their families from eight countries around the world, from the moment they open their eyes until the end of their busy day. Beautifully illustrated with colour photographs. Includes Sasha, Linh and Cidinha, who are featured in *Photo Opportunities Science*.
Frances Lincoln in association with Oxfam, 1999

W is for World
Kathryn Cave
A book for young children illustrated with photos from over twenty countries.
Frances Lincoln, Oxfam 1998

USING PHOTOGRAPHS

Photo Opportunities Maths
The second in Oxfam's Photo Opportunities series, this photopack brings a global dimension to maths activities. Closely linked to the National Curricula of England, Scotland and Wales, it features activities for the maths lesson, each based on a stimulating photo taken overseas. Contains 12 A4 colour photos, a teacher's book and a colour poster.

Photo Opportunities 2000
A new edition of this best-selling photopack, with 22 A5 colour photos which show people from around the world going about their everyday life. The teacher's book gives guidance on using photographs in the classroom, and includes easy-to-follow activities. Particularly relevant for English and literacy.
Oxfam, 2000

Your World, My World
Incorporating some of the characters featured in *Wake up, World!*, this photopack addresses issues in the PSE and PSD curricula, helping children to explore what makes up their special identity, the importance of family and friends and their role in helping others. The teacher's booklet contains detailed background information on the children and countries featured. Contains 24 A4 photocards, teacher's booklet and A1 colour poster.
Oxfam, 2001

Wake up, World! CD ROM
Based on *Wake up, World!*, which compares the lives of children around the world, this resource features interactive, cross-curricular activities for young children and comes with a book of teacher's notes, activity sheets and a poster. Themes explored include water, transport, climate and school. It relates to numeracy, geography and ICT.
Anglia Multimedia, 2000

Sarah Errington / Oxfam

Crispin Hughes / Oxfam

Joel Chizane / Oxfam

Julio Etchart / Oxfam

Oxfam